CORE LANGUAGE SKILLS

Antonyms and Synonyms

Kara Murray

PowerKiDS
press.

New York

Published in 2015 by The Rosen Publishing Group, Inc.
29 East 21st Street, New York, NY 10010

First Edition

Editor: Sarah Machajewski
Book Design: Reann Nye

Photo Credits: Cover Vadim.Petrov/Shutterstock.com; p. 5 Olesya Feketa/Shutterstock.com; p. 7 Bob Elsdale/The Image Bank/Getty Images; p. 8 iko/Shutterstock.com; p. 9 (dog) Jari Hindstroem/Shutterstock.com; p. 9 (cat) Eric Isselee/Shutterstock.com; pp. 11, 17 (pencil) Julia Ivantsova/Shutterstock.com; p. 13 Michael H/Digital Vision/Getty Images; p. 15 (both runners) Maridav/Shutterstock.com; p. 19 Stockbyte/Stockbyte/Getty Images; p. 20 Alexander Cherednichenko/Shutterstock.com; p. 21 Monkey Business Images/Shutterstock.com.

Library of Congress Cataloging-in-Publication Data

Murray, Kara.
Antonyms and synonyms / by Kara Murray.
p. cm. — (Core language skills)
Includes index.
ISBN 978-1-4777-7357-4 (pbk.)
ISBN 978-1-4777-7358-1 (6-pack)
ISBN 978-1-4777-7356-7 (library binding)
1. English language — Synonyms and antonyms — Juvenile literature. I. Murray, Kara. II. Title.
PE1591.M87 2015
428.1—d23

Manufactured in the United States of America

CPSIA Compliance Information: Batch #CW15PK: For Further Information contact Rosen Publishing, New York, New York at 1-800-237-9932

CONTENTS

THE RIGHT WORDS FOR THE JOB

Have you ever sat down to write something, but couldn't think of the right words to use? This can happen when you're speaking, too. Writers choose words that fit the message they're trying to tell us. Luckily, there are many words to choose from, and they all have certain meanings.

Choosing the right words is an important language skill. Antonyms and synonyms are parts of language that help us with this. Antonyms are words that mean the opposite of each other. Synonyms are words that have the same or similar meanings.

Figure It Out

What is the difference between antonyms and synonyms?

Find the answer to this question and the others in this book on page 22.

It's easy to pick the right words when you understand antonyms and synonyms!

USING ANTONYMS AND SYNONYMS

Antonyms and synonyms help **describe** things. Antonyms help us describe opposites, such as an elephant and a mouse. An elephant is big, and a mouse is small. "Big" and "small" are antonyms.

Synonyms help us describe something without using the same word over and over. They can be swapped out of a sentence without changing its meaning. If you feel happy, you don't always have to use the word "happy." You can also say you feel glad or cheerful. "Happy," "glad," and "cheerful" have similar meanings, so they're synonyms.

Figure It Out

Can you find the synonyms in the following sentences? "I like the way my mom talks. She speaks very softly."

The elephant and mouse shown here are total opposites. We can use antonyms to describe them.

ALL ABOUT ANTONYMS

It's not hard to come up with antonyms. The opposite of something is usually easy to guess, especially when a word has a clear opposite. "Wet" and "dry" are words with clear antonyms. "Wet" is the clear opposite of "dry," just as "dry" is the clear opposite of "wet."

Are you unsure about when to use an antonym and when to use a synonym? Ask yourself if you're describing things that are different or things that are alike.

But hold on! It's not always that simple. Some words have many antonyms. The opposite of "big" is "small," but that's not the only one. "Tiny" and "little" are opposites of "big," too.

Figure It Out

"Big" is just one antonym for "small." Can you think of other antonyms for the word "small"?

MAKING ANTONYMS WITH PREFIXES

Picture this. You sit down to write an **essay**. You want to include antonyms, but you don't know many off the top of your head. Don't worry! You can make antonyms in no time at all. Sometimes, all you have to do is add a **prefix** to a **root word**.

A prefix goes at the beginning of a word and changes its meaning. Many prefixes turn words into their opposite. One prefix that does this is "un-." If you want to make an antonym for "happy," simply add "un-," and now you have "unhappy." See how easy it is?

Figure It Out

The prefix "mis-" turns a word into its antonym. If you add "mis-" to the word "understand," you make "misunderstand." Can you figure out the meaning of the new word?

Prefixes Make Opposites!

un-	dis-	im-
able | unable	believe | disbelieve	pure | impure
funny | unfunny	appear | disappear	possible | impossible
loved | unloved	agree | disagree	polite | impolite

Adding a prefix is an easy way to make antonyms, but be careful. It doesn't work all the time. For example, "unbig" is definitely not the opposite of big. In fact, it's not even a word at all!

STUDYING SYNONYMS

Have you ever found yourself saying "What's another word for...?" You may not have known it then, but you were looking for a synonym. Most words have many synonyms.

You may wonder why there are so many words that mean the same thing. Well, it's simple. Synonyms give your writing **variety**. You have many choices, so you don't always have to use the same word. This keeps your writing and speech from being boring or **repetitive**. Plus, knowing synonyms is a great way to build your **vocabulary**.

Figure It Out

Look at the following sentences. The word "cook" is used a lot. Can you think of synonyms that would make these sentences more interesting?
"I know how to cook spaghetti. I cook it a lot. It's fun to cook spaghetti."

Using the same words over and over can lose your readers' attention. Using synonyms will make sure you keep it!

SHADES OF MEANING

Each word in our language has its own special meaning. It's important to remember that synonyms are *not* the same word. They're very similar, but their meanings are often slightly different.

For example, the words "running" and "jogging" are synonyms. They both describe a way of moving your body. However, "running" means moving very quickly. "Jogging" means moving quickly but not as quickly as running. If you see someone running, you can't always say that he or she is jogging, too.

Figure It Out

Can you think of a synonym to **replace** "house" in the following sentence? "My grandma's house is far away."

The best way to decide if a synonym makes sense is to think about how the word makes you feel. Does that feeling match what you want to say? If it doesn't feel right, it's probably not the right synonym to use.

TOOLS OF THE TRADE

The English language has a huge number of words. It's impossible to know them all. There's one tool you can use to help you unlock the world of synonyms and antonyms. It's a thesaurus (thuh-SOHR-uhs)!

A thesaurus is a book that lists words and their synonyms and antonyms. Writers use a thesaurus to find the perfect word for what they're trying to say. Imagine you want to replace the word "jump" with a synonym. A thesaurus may list "leap," "hop," or "spring." Choose the one that fits your writing best, and ta-da! You've just used a thesaurus to improve your writing.

Figure It Out

The following sentence uses the word "angry." Does replacing it with "mad" change its meaning?

"My parents get angry when I fight with my sister."

The Core Language Skills
Thesaurus

word	synonyms	antonyms
bad	awful, rotten, terrible	great, good, super
funny	laughable, silly, witty	serious, unfunny
smart	bright, clever, wise	dumb, stupid
tired	beat, sleepy, weary	energized, fresh
weird	odd, strange, unusual	normal, usual

TEST IT OUT

Now that you know all about antonyms and synonyms, it's time to put them to use. Try including them in your next essay or school **project**. Sometimes the first word that comes to mind may be one you've already used. This is a good time to use a synonym.

Antonyms can come in handy while writing, too. They're very helpful in **opinion** pieces. Try describing the opposite of what you want before telling readers what you *actually* want. If readers can see both sides, they may agree with yours!

Figure It Out

"Terrible" and "wonderful" are antonyms. So are "hate" and "love." Do they help you understand the writer's opinion in the following sentences? "Winter is terrible. I hate the cold and snow! Summer is wonderful. I love when it's hot out!"

If you come across a new word while you're reading, look for clues around it to help you figure out its meaning. It may mean the same thing as a word you already know.

A WRITER'S TOOLBOX

Knowing how to find the perfect synonym or antonym—and when to use it—is part of becoming a good writer. Great writers, though, take care to find the right word. Don't pick just any word without truly knowing what it means. Remember, sometimes the best word is not the biggest word!

Figure It Out

Can you pick out the antonyms and synonyms in the following sentence? "A little crow sits in a big tree near my house. Its caws are very noisy. They're especially loud in the morning!"

Finding the right words to tell others your ideas will bring your writing to life. It's always good to learn new words. Learning synonyms and antonyms gives you many new tools for your writing toolbox!

FIGURE IT OUT ANSWERS

Page 4: Antonyms are opposites. Synonyms are words that mean the same thing or have very similar meanings.

Page 6: "Talks" and "speaks" are synonyms.

Page 9: "Huge" and "large" are antonyms for "small."

Page 10: "Misunderstand" means "to not understand."

Page 12: Synonyms are "prepare" and "make." The new sentences read, "I know how to cook spaghetti. I prepare it a lot. It's fun to make spaghetti."

Page 14: "Home" is one synonym for "house."

Page 16: No, the meaning is the same. "Mad" and "angry" can be used to say the same thing.

Page 18: Yes. The writer likes summer. They don't like winter.

Page 20: "Little" and "big" are antonyms. "Noisy" and "loud" are synonyms.

GLOSSARY

describe (dih-SCRYB) To tell about.

essay (EH-say) A short piece of writing.

opinion (uh-PIHN-yuhn) What you think about something.

prefix (PREE-fihks) A group of letters that goes at the beginning of a word and changes its meaning.

project (PRAH-jehkt) A task worked on by students to learn something.

repetitive (rih-PEH-tuh-tihv) Said or done over and over.

replace (rih-PLAYS) To take the place of.

root word (ROOT WUHRD) The simplest form of a word.

variety (vuh-RY-uh-tee) A number of differences within one group.

vocabulary (voh-KAA-byuh-lehr-ee) The words you know.

INDEX

WEBSITES

Due to the changing nature of Internet links, PowerKids Press has developed an online list of websites related to the subject of this book. This site is updated regularly. Please use this link to access the list: www.powerkidslinks.com/cls/ansy